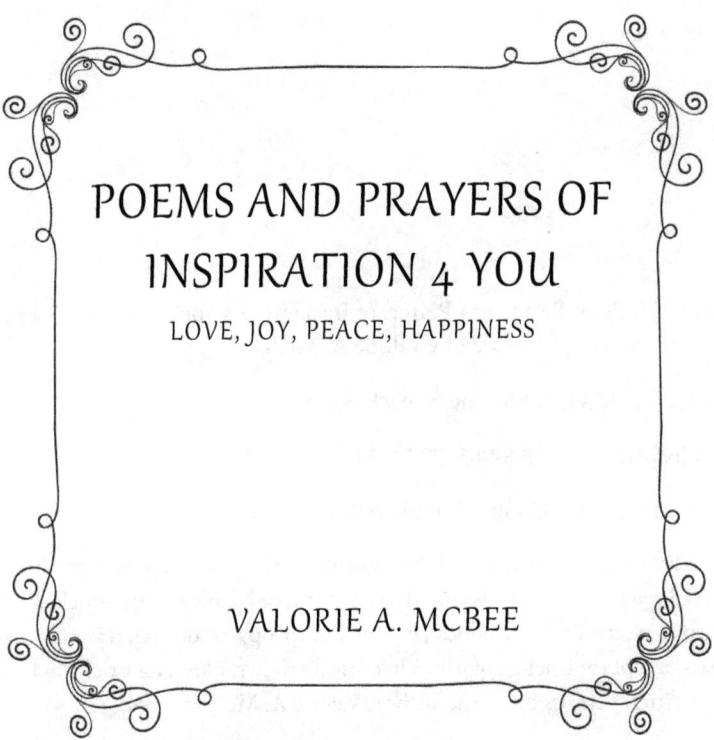

POEMS AND PRAYERS OF
INSPIRATION 4 YOU

LOVE, JOY, PEACE, HAPPINESS

VALORIE A. MCBEE

ACKNOWLEDGEMENTS

First and foremost, I honor and praise God for blessing me with the words of inspiration to share with others. Thank you to my husband, Douglas, and sons, Brian and Michael, and my daughter-in-law, Shinell, for your constant love and support. Thanks to my brother James, and cousin Regina for always keeping in touch and being there with a listening ear. I appreciate the love and support of my sisters in-law Linda, Denise, Ophelia, Helene Rose and Yvonne, my brother-in-law, Richard, all of my nieces and nephews and other family members and friends. I am also grateful for the support of my pastor, Rev. Dr. Roscoe Cooper, III and the Rising Mt. Zion Church family, the Spratley Allen missionaries, the VOICE newsletter staff, the Ministries of the Baptist General Convention and the Lott Carey Baptist Foreign Mission and the St. Paul A.M.E. Church family, the Believers Friendship Circle, my longtime friends of the PTA, the sisters of SUITS, and the James Rivers Writers and a host of relatives, friends and co-workers whose love and support were gifted to me over the years. Several poems were originally composed by way of special requests or for special occasions. For instance, A Perspective on Marriage was composed for my son Brian and his wife Shinell on their wedding day. My daughter-in-law's mother, Elvira Switzer requested a poem for their Deaconess program with the theme of God's Helpers. The Peacekeeper was inspired by my son Michael. A Tribute to Those Who Serve was originally composed for Deacon Mary Kemp, the editor-in-chief of our church's newsletter. A Prayer for You was written to encourage a long-time friend, Deacon Evelena Carter, who was the caregiver for her father. A Brother was composed at the request of a friend, Karen Brown, during the passing of her brother. A Healing Prayer was composed for a co-worker, D. Morris, when her relative was facing health problems. When We Meet Again was inspired by my husband and sons and written in memory of my dear

Big Ma (Blanche Carpenter Rogers). I appreciate LaTesha Barnes and Vivian Minor's talent, time and effort. I am grateful for Dr. Kimberly A. Matthews who recommended me to Kim at KWE Publishing. Thank you, Kim Eley, my publisher, whose patience easily matched that of Job's. I appreciate your understanding and most cheerful mannerism.

To the reader, these poems were written to encourage and inspire you. May God bless you all.

DEDICATION

I dedicate these words of inspiration to my most loving and dearest grands, Omari and Mykhia. I pray that you will be abundantly blessed, and receive much love, joy, peace, happiness, and inspiration in your heart to pass on to others, for you will be inspired when you inspire others.

IN LOVING MEMORY OF LOVED ONES WHO UNDOUBTEDLY HAD AN INFLUENCE ON MY LIFE AND WERE AN INSPIRATION TO ME

My grandmother, Blanche Carpenter Rogers (Big Ma) who taught me poems to recite in church (St. Paul A.M.E.), my beautiful Mom, Annie Sturgis Teagle, and step-father, William Teagle, who wanted only the best for us; my brothers Wilbert, the other family poet; Milton, the avid reader; and Frank, highly intelligent, yet very comical; my "rhyming words" and storytelling Uncle Billy (Walter Rogers); my cousins Big John (Samuel White), the artistic one, and Annie Mae White Snead, whom I loved to visit in Delaware at the beach. Aunt Emma Rogers Gunter, who was always there with love and care; my caring mother-in law and father-in law, Richard and Ernestine McBee; my quiet yet strong sister-in-law Doris and her husband Charles; and my cousin Alice Rogers Ames, and niece Nita (Bennetta Sturgis Lord), my sisters in spirit.

TABLE OF CONTENTS

INTRODUCTION

The title of this book, *Poems and Prayers of Inspiration 4 You*, originated from the name of a business that I planned to start after my retirement from the public school system. I developed somewhat of a business plan that included being a coordinator as well as a speaker for programs, workshops, and special events. However, before acquiring my business license, I needed to come up with a name; and since my youngest son was a business major, I mentioned to him about a name. We discussed Inspirational Treasures for You; therefore, being young and innovative, he suggested using the number "4" instead of "for." Yet, I felt that the number "4" in this case should represent a more meaningful connotation and concluded that the "4" would represent Love, Joy, Peace, and Happiness. Consequently, my business name became Inspirational Treasures 4 You; hence, the title of this book, *Poems and Prayers of Inspiration 4 You: Love, Joy, Peace, Happiness.*

The idea of Love, Joy, Peace, Happiness brings to my mind, "Inspiration." It is my belief that each one of us, from every walk of life, at one time or another, yearns to be inspired and to have our spirit uplifted. People throughout the world who were in distress during the 2020 Covid-19 pandemic need hope and inspiration. Persons who lost jobs, homes and businesses, the sick and shut-in, the caregivers of the sick, first responders, our teachers, faith leaders and other leaders, and people in all types of service everywhere, all need prayer every now and then. People who are concerned about the economy, the environment, their children's future, and many who are stressed from the trials and tribulations of everyday life, I believe, could use some inspiration. Nonetheless, it is my hope that you will be blessed in some way, shape, form, or fashion (one of my grandmother's favorite sayings) by one of my inspirational poems or prayers.

Here's wishing you...

LOVE—May your heart overflow with God's agape love, grace and mercy as you, in turn, love and care for others.

JOY—May your heart be filled with joy as you inspire another.

PEACE—May you experience peace in your soul knowing that you reached out with kindness to someone else.

HAPPINESS—May you experience happiness along with many other blessings during this life's journey.

THE ORIGIN OF THE WORD "POETRY"

"Late Middle English: from Medieval Latin poetria, from Latin poeta 'poet.' In early use, the word sometimes referred to creative literature in general" (Oxford Living Dictionaries).

My Personal Experience in Inspirational Writings and Poetry

As a child growing up in a small town on the Eastern Shore, I remember my grandmother teaching me poems to recite in church even before I could read. Big Ma, as she was fondly called, would adorn me in dresses of lace, ribbons and can-can slips (crinolines), stand me before the congregation and I would recite a beautiful poem and then take a deep bow. It's been one of my most favorite childhood memories.

I also remember my grandmother encouraging my brothers and older cousins to read the newspaper comics to me and my other younger cousins. She often read the Bible to all of us. My uncle and one of my brothers were good with "rhyming words"; they simply made-up poems in the spur of the moment. I was amazed because my uncle was also a great storyteller. However, once I learned to read on my own, I would read and write to my heart's content. I did not keep any of my earlier poems from childhood, I simply composed for the fun of it. In college, I enjoyed writing papers on different topics and quite often typed a famous quote or short poem at the end (but not necessarily for extra credit). I read poetry and other books to our two sons when they were young and now to our grand-children. What a blessing!

Later in life, I began composing poetry to inspire others and have composed poems upon special requests for different occasions.

I became quite serious about publishing my inspirational writings and poetry after having the honor of helping my brother when he published his book of poetry. I have always loved reading different types of literature, reciting, and listening to poetry; hence, composing inspirational poems has become one of my favorite past-times. My philosophy about poetry is that a poem is a play on words and can be about pretty much...anything.

A POEM ABOUT ANYTHING

A poem can be composed about anything;
just seek and allow your heart to bring...
the words to mind and mindfulness you'll see,
will create the thoughts of who you would like to be...
A Poet, of course,
if that's the desire of your heart for sure.

God, I thank You for Your Holy Word, and for all the poetic and wisdom books in the scriptures: Job, Psalms, Proverbs, Ecclesiastes, and the Songs of Solomon. And I thank You, Dear Lord, for the words You have given us as Your people so that we may inspire others in verse, rhyme, song, sonnets, and all the positive and inspirational forms of word usage.

INSPIRATION 4 YOU
Love, Joy, Peace, Happiness

This is to inspire you, uplift your spirit and encourage you.
This verse of inspiration for you may be long overdue.
Our hearts may be heavy, our minds could be cloudy,
And our bodies may be wracked with pain.
Yet, we are blessed because of the goodness and mercies
we've gained.
For God so loved the world that He gave His only begotten son,
And we as His children must run this race until we've won—
The Victory.
By being loving, reaching out and helping one another,
We can make a difference if we only pull together.
Faith, hope, love—the Bible says love is the greatest of all.
If we just love and care for each other,
Will we falter or fall?
Quite the contrary, we will be inspired and uplifted,
With love in our hearts, we are already gifted.
One step at a time is all that's required, or choose a plan of action...
Reach out, inspire and uplift others
with love and compassion.
Return to the one who gave, pass on to another,
or simply pay forward.
Just continue to reach out to another
and faithfully march onward.
And as we journey through life and gracefully run this race,
We will reap the miraculous benefit of
God's marvelous mercy and amazing grace.

Inspiration 4 You
Love, Joy, Peace, Happiness

THE PEACEKEEPER
Inspired by My Son

Peace is seeking, pleasing God.

Peace is love for all,
Great or small.

Peace is watching a newborn baby sleeping, peacefully.
Peace is returning a smile to another human being, smiling sweetly.

Peace is meditation, quiet moments, few thoughts.
Peace is a prayer, a spiritual connection from deep within the
soul and heart.

Peace is nature—a flower, sunny skies, stars in the sky
on a clear night,
or simply watching birds in flight.

So finding and keeping peace begins within me.
And as you can see,
You can be a peacekeeper too
When peace begins within you.

Oh God, help us to become peacekeepers.
The evil spirit is lurking, even devouring purposefully.
People are hurting, scouring aimlessly,
They have no peace.

Peace begins with one soul, and it flows...
Into the family, into the world.
The soul, the family, the world is lost without peace.
I employ you to become a seeker of peace.

Find Peace—
And Become a Peacekeeper.

A TRIBUTE TO THOSE WHO SERVE

This poem was originally composed in honor of our editor-in-chief who served for 20 years on our church's newsletter staff. Now, I dedicate this poem to all who serve and help others in any positive or noble capacity.

You are a mighty human being designed and created by God.
Your love and care for others is Christ-like in so many ways.
The Lord has blessed you with the gift of excellence,
To exhibit throughout your days.
Your service may touch those near or far,
What an extraordinary person you are.
One of positivity, truth, understanding, and wisdom,
You are certainly a catalyst for building God's kingdom.
Oh quiet, yet focused and steady laborer,
Through the Lord's strength and guidance you are able.
And what a blessing you are to us all,
For indeed, you have answered God's call.
So remain loving and caring, faithful, steadfast, and true.
Because today, through God's grace, we are celebrating YOU!

INSPIRATION 4 YOU, THE CAREGIVER
Love, Joy, Peace, Happiness

Years ago, I became the long-distance caregiver for my elderly uncle and my cousin who had cancer. My husband and I traveled to help them whenever and however we could. Years later, I also became the long-distance caregiver for one of my brothers. Oftentimes, the role of caregiving falls upon us without notice. Although we may assume the responsibility with love and care, it can take a physical, mental, emotional, and a financial toll upon us.

Therefore, within my spirit I felt compelled to do something to help others who take care of loved ones. I approached my pastor about my willingness to help other caregivers; he was very supportive. Serving as our church's missionary president at the time, I then presented an idea to our missionaries about inviting caregivers to our annual Christmas luncheon; they were so excited. We invited speakers from health organizations and caregivers to share their experiences. The program was also blessed with prayer, music, scripture, and delicious food. We held The Caregivers Fellowship Luncheon annually for 10 years. We were planning to include cancer survivors as part of our program before the 2020 COVID-19 Pandemic forced us to cancel. We trust that God will continue to bless us and we look forward to providing this program again.

Dear God,
We thank You for all Your blessings,
For life's trials, tribulations, and lessons.

Dear Caregiver,
Whatever your plight, whatever the test,
Do whatever you can; just do your best.
And God will surely do the rest.
Stay encouraged, inspired, and uplifted.
Hearts are inspired by God,
Therefore, we are gifted
To love, assist, and encourage one another,
Most certainly so, dear sister and brother.
So pray, pray, pray,
For guidance and strength throughout the day.
God will direct your path,
And help you find your way.

GOD'S HELPERS

This poem was written at the request of my daughter-in-law's mother whose Deaconess Ministry was sponsoring a program at their church; their theme was "God's Helpers."

Let us be thankful that God wants to use us
to glorify His Kingdom.
And in our willingness to serve God, by serving others,
We will receive through grace, the wisdom...
To help one another—my dear sister and brother.
To lend a helping hand—for there is a great demand.
There are those in need of prayer and our unconditional love,
For God's grace and agape love is truly from above.
To greet the people we meet from day to day,
As we so journey along this life's way.
To offer a word of kindness and inspiration,
For we are all a part of God's awesome creation.
Each one is blessed with a gift whether great or small,
And God will grant us what we need when we are called.
Each one of us was created for a purpose;
To carry out the Master's plan.
Therefore, pray for guidance and then do the best you can.
Serve with humbleness, open-heartedness, and love,
And then your miracles and blessings will flow from God above.

A PRAYER FOR YOU

"A Prayer for You" was originally written with a very close friend in mind who unselfishly served as the long-distance caregiver for her father.

As time passes on and we look back over the years,
God has truly blessed us through all trials, tribulations, and tears.
So when we try to do our best for our loved ones,
And weariness begins to take its toll,
God, we thank You in advance for stepping in to take control.
Thank You for providing the wisdom, understanding,
and guidance on decisions.
God, we claim Your gifts
of physical, emotional, and financial provisions.
Thank You for giving our families the strength to endure,
And God, we give You the honor and praise forevermore.
Amen, Amen, Amen.

A PRAYER FOR SOMEONE ELSE
Love, Joy, Peace, Happiness

Dear God, I pray this prayer for someone else,
Not that I don't need prayer myself.
I care deeply for others I meet along the way,
And I pray that You will bestow a blessing upon them today.
Bestow upon them Your Love, Joy, Peace, and Happiness.
Grant them the power and wisdom to receive it all with gladness.
I pray for their family, their friends, and their community.
I pray that you will bless them abundantly,
and give them hope and unity.
Dear God, whatever their need,
Be it a breakthrough or just a good deed,
Be with them today,
In Jesus' name I pray.
Amen, Amen, Amen.

HONORING GOD BY BEING FILLED WITH COMPASSION, KINDNESS, GENTLENESS, HUMILITY, PATIENCE, LOVE

It was an honor and a privilege to compose this poem for an event that was sponsored by our District Area A missionaries of the Baptist General Convention of Virginia—Women's Division. The "Tea" was held in April 2014 and prizes were offered for the three best decorated tables. Missionaries from each participating church including the Rising Mount Zion Baptist Church- Spratley Allen Missionary Circle adorned their tables with beautiful tablecloths, floral arrangements, and colorful teacups as they served delicious tea, dainty sandwiches, and delectable desserts. The theme for the program was "Honoring God By Being Filled With Compassion, Kindness, Gentleness, Humility, Patience, Love," hence the reason I chose to entitle this poem. It was a truly blessed occasion; our spirits were uplifted with heartfelt prayer, scripture, poetry, songs of praise, and an excellent keynote speaker.

Dear God,
Thank You for life, for Your guidance, understanding, and wisdom.
We are truly blessed, and anticipate the coming of Your kingdom.
To my sisters and brothers, we can honor God
With every good deed and action
By showing love, kindness, patience, humility,
gentleness, and compassion.
We honor God, when love is embedded in our heart.
And to be filled with love is a good and noble start.
For only then can we dwell on kindly thoughts
and a positive way of seeing.
And so we honor God when these virtues
become a natural way of being.
We could uplift someone's spirit,
By giving them a smile, a hug, or lovingly say,
"You look nice today, I love you; can I help you along your way?"
Honoring God is when we possess humility and meekness.
No, my brothers and sisters, this is not a sign of weakness.
For according to the book of Matthew,
Blessed are the meek for they shall inherit the earth.
So humility is definitely not a curse,
Humility reflects a strong, yet quiet and gentle spirit,
With a godly purpose, that is gracefully exhibited.
Therefore, we should seek to become wise leaders,
And certainly not power seekers.
We must develop patience; as patience is a virtue.
Patience helps us to wait for the godly way, tis true.
We wait for God's healing in body, mind, and spirit
As we pray throughout the day.
We do the best we can, and wait for God
to direct our path along life's way.

Being filled with gentleness and compassion shows that we care.
We appreciate, respect, and love one another, and ourselves;
That's my prayer.
Love, kindness, humility, gentleness,
patience, and compassion,
Are virtues that enable us to grow, and exhibit behavior
of godly ways and actions.
We've heard these words many times before,
And by BEING virtuous we can open the door—
For HONORING GOD.

A PERSPECTIVE ON MARRIAGE

This poem was originally composed as a tribute to my son and his wife on their wedding day. I now dedicate this poem to anyone who is planning to marry or is already married.

Marriage is the union of two people,
the unison of two hearts in love.
The love that we have for one another is a blessed gift from above.
God bestows this gift upon each and every heart,
At the beginning of life, from the very start.
The love that God has for each one of us,
agape love is unconditional,
It is true, faithful, and not situational.
Marriage requires love, passion, consideration,
respect, and commitment.
It also requires sacrifice, perseverance, but no resentment.
There will be life's trials, hurts, and tribulations,
But you remain prayerful, faithful, patient,
and hold on to determination.
Marriage is also happiness, joy, laughter, and bliss.
Little hurt feelings can be eased with an apology, hug, or a kiss.
Do seek wisdom; the book of Proverbs is one good source.
Take others' good advice, but even then with a grain of salt.
Have fun, enjoy life, but remain prayerful in everything,
Pray for and with each other.
Most of all, keep God in your life and remain true to one another.
These are my words of encouragement for you,
Do take heed, for they are given with my love for you.
So today, we celebrate your marriage and the unity of our families—

What a blessing!
And we truly thank God for all of life's blessings
and love everlasting.

A BASKET OF BLESSINGS—FAMILY

This poem is dedicated to all families.

Families are blessings that come from above.
Admiration we have for one another, surely it's out of love.
Memories are precious, so we hold them close to our heart.
Inspiration we give to uplift and impart.
Love is a gift that comes through God's agape love from above,
You are very special, so I send you my love.

A PRAYER FOR MOTHERS

This poem was composed and printed in our church's newsletter (The Rising Mt. Zion Voice Newsletter) to honor mothers on Mother's Day.

Dear God, we pray for mothers everywhere.
We pray that You will keep them in Your care.
Bless their children from the youngest to the oldest,
whether they are near or far.
We ask that You direct their paths
and guide them as a shining star.
We pray that You grant all mothers strength, patience, wisdom,
and love.
God, Your agape love is a blessing for all mothers
throughout the world.
We thank You Dear God and give Your name
all the honor, praise, and glory.
Amen.

GRANDCHILDREN—BLESSINGS OF JOY

Grandchildren are blessings of joy
How precious can they be...
For they are our future, you see,
In all the earth and eternity.
Grandchildren are thought-provoking, kind, loving, and true.
They are free-spirited, adventurous, brave, and bold too.
But oh, how the years fly by,
Remember how you sometimes used to cry,
When you visited during the summer
with Grandma and Grandpa,
And missed Mommy and Daddy at bedtime
when the night was nigh?
Yet as we began reading favorite bedtime stories to you,
Your little faces would light up and glow with wonderment; tis true.
Sometimes we would make plans for the following week.
And prayers were always repeated before falling off to sleep.
On Sundays we attended church
to seek spiritual growth and Christ-like ways.
We visited the library, ran through the park,
had fun at the water splash on those hot days.
Don't forget the museums, cook-outs
and games in the backyard too.
And the visits with family and friends that were long overdue.
Indeed, grandchildren are blessings from heaven above;
We are thankful for you and send you our love,
We are so proud to see you blossom and grow.
We can rely on our faith in God and know,
That your achievements
and accomplishments will be blessed from above.

Grandchildren—Our Future, Our Hope,
and Blessings of Joy and Love.

A BROTHER

This poem was composed at the request of a friend who is a co-editor of our church newsletter. Her brother passed and she asked me to compose a poem pertaining to a brother. It was printed on the back of his program on March 5, 2020. She said when she read this verse that it brought her to tears.

A brother is sent from heaven above,
A special someone for us to love.
A brother may be a husband, a father, uncle, or friend,
A son who is there 'till the very end.
As God is our refuge in times of trouble,
The Almighty may send us protection,
Through a faithful and trustworthy brother.
With the Lord's help, a brother can take a righteous stand,
And more often than not, will lend a helping hand.
One who is encouraging and loving in a time of need,
A brother is a treasure and a blessing, indeed.

WE WILL MEET AGAIN

In 2010, the church where my grandmother was a devoted member (St. Paul A.M.E.) celebrated their 144th anniversary, and this poem was printed on the memorial page of the program in honor of my grandmother, my uncle, and other family members.

What memories we have of our loved ones,
The most precious are dear to our hearts.
To look back on times past,
And to feel confident at last,
That we will see one another again
On another shore, in another time and space.
To know that God has prepared
A most heavenly place,
For our meeting again.
Oh yes, as promised, it will be
A most joyous occasion, you'll see,
When we meet again,
When we meet again.

ON HEALING

Do not fear, for I am with you; do not be afraid, for I am your God;
I will strengthen you, I will help you, I will uphold you with my
victorious right hand. Isaiah 41:10 (NRSV)

This was the scripture that my son texted me in May 2019 when I was preparing to undergo cancer surgery for the third time. In 2008, before my first surgical procedure, my brother advised me to read Hebrews, chapter 11. I am a living testament to God's faithfulness and healing.

However, the original story behind my healing prayer poem began one Tuesday morning on January 6, 2009, when a co-worker confided in me that her niece was experiencing some medical issues. I could sense in my spirit that she was deeply concerned and I was touched by what she told me so I composed this healing prayer/poem for her. It was approximately a year after my first lumpectomy for stage 0 breast cancer.

Over the years, I have composed a number of poems and inspirational writings, yet when I originally composed and emailed this particular writing to my co-worker on that day in 2009, I had no idea that I would be reading my own poem to and for myself years later. During my second experience with cancer, I learned the virtue of real patience, that healing takes time, and my faith and spirituality increased. I am now experiencing a profound appreciation for God's love, grace, and mercy.

When I was a young child, my grandmother (Big Ma), taught me poems to recite in church and she often read the Bible to her grand and great-grandchildren. However, when I learned to read on my own, reading poetry and the Bible became a wonderful pastime for me. And while attending college, "The Bible as Literature" was one of my most thought-provoking classes. I now discover a deeper meaning when *reading, reflecting, and meditating on sacred writings. And I pray more often throughout the day, for self and others.*

Words cannot express my thankfulness to God for the love, care, and support of my husband, sons, other family members, pastor and church family, friends, and medical staff who have assisted me during this journey.

For anyone who is experiencing physical, mental, emotional, or even spiritual challenges, I pray that this healing prayer/poem will help provide some consolation. I pray that it will uplift your spirit and give you hope and inspiration; and that you will experience God's everlasting love despite what you may be going through.

A HEALING PRAYER

DEAR GOD,
I come before You this day,
Knowing that Your will is Your way.
Yet, I ask in the name of Jesus,
That You will place in me...HEALING,
HEALING of my spirit, mind, and body.

I pray for HEALING throughout my being,
to claim, possess, and feel Your goodness.
HEALING in my heart, to feel
Your Love, Grace, Mercy, and Peace,
To know in my spirit that You are an awesome God
and that there is nothing that You cannot do.

DEAR GOD, I ask for HEALING in my thought process;
To meditate on Your word, to think on positive things,
To think on love, goodness, and righteousness,
And as a result of my thinking,
I pray that my ways and actions will be pleasing in Your sight.

I ask for HEALING in my body.
I claim the physical well-being of every part of my body right now.
For You made me in Your image
and I know that You will place Your HEALING Hand upon me.
I know that my body is a temple and I ask for
Your guidance on its care.

DEAR GOD, I thank YOU for
YOUR AWESOME HEALING POWER.

I LOVE THE LORD

I love the Lord, the One and only Almighty God,
A God who is righteous, loving, and true,
The One who loves unconditionally, me and you.

I love the Lord, the One and only Almighty God.
A God whose Word conveyed in truth will light the way,
The One who is powerful and infinite,
a deliverer of joy and peace,
A comforter and healer each and every day.

I love the Lord, the One and only Almighty God,
The One who is Holy, merciful, kind, and faithful,
Thank You Lord, for I am truly blessed and most grateful.
To God Be the Glory,
Amen.

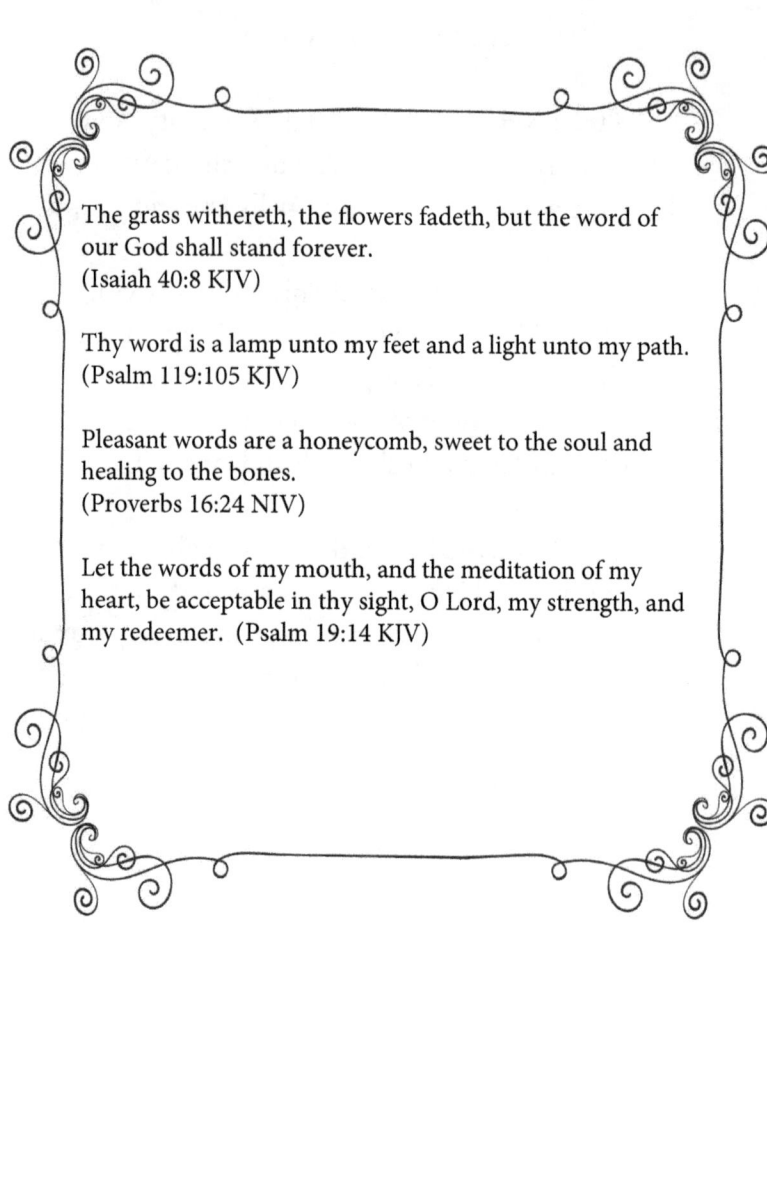

The grass withereth, the flowers fadeth, but the word of
our God shall stand forever.
(Isaiah 40:8 KJV)

Thy word is a lamp unto my feet and a light unto my path.
(Psalm 119:105 KJV)

Pleasant words are a honeycomb, sweet to the soul and
healing to the bones.
(Proverbs 16:24 NIV)

Let the words of my mouth, and the meditation of my
heart, be acceptable in thy sight, O Lord, my strength, and
my redeemer. (Psalm 19:14 KJV)

WORDS

Words seldom evade me.
In fact, words imbue my thought process,
And flow into and through my mind,
like water seeping into some kind
of opening.
Yet, I often find
that I'm searching for a particular word,
One that I may have heard,
Somewhere along life's way.
Or sometimes words just come into play,
Into my mind, my heart, my spirit.
And they flow like a beautiful lyric...
Oh, let us sing praises unto the Lord,
As we express our love to God on one accord.
Words have meanings so we must be careful
To not hurt one another,
but to be loving and kind and oh yes, cheerful.
Notably, the "Old English" words have a particular flair,
Like a butterfly fluttering through the air.
As the Old English word "thee" in the old hymn,
"I Need Thee Every Hour..."
It's a plea to God, our Savior Who holds all power.

A SIMPLE PRAYER OF GRATITUDE

A simple prayer of gratitude will go a long way.
It will get you through the night and certainly through the day.
I thank You Dear God for others that I meet along the way.
I pray that You will bestow Your many blessings upon them this day.

My motto: Helping others from day to day,
As I journey along life's way.

May you be blessed with much love, joy, peace, and happiness.

ABOUT THE AUTHOR

Valorie A. McBee is a native of Philadelphia and was reared on the Eastern Shore of Virginia. Valorie attended Norfolk State College (University) where she met her then future husband; they are blessed with children and grandchildren after 48 years of marriage. Valorie completed her education by graduating from Virginia Commonwealth University with a Bachelor's Degree in Interdisciplinary Studies focusing on Family Culture from a Socio-educational Perspective. She is listed in the 65th volume of Who's Who Among Students in American Universities and Colleges.

Over the years, Valorie has served as president and/or committee chair of several organizations. She has been a member or has volunteered with numerous community organizations. She is an active missionary member, and serves on her church newsletter staff. For several years, Valorie was the long-distance caregiver for her uncle and brother. With the support of her pastor and missionary members she initiated a caregivers program for those who take care of loved ones. Valorie has been employed by federal and state governments as well as several public school systems. She also worked at the university where she later graduated. She holds a real estate sales license (inactive); and while her children were young, she became a stay-at-home mom and started a home-based business; she acquired a business license, worked as a federal independent contractor and sold residential real estate. Years later, Valorie returned to full-time employment with the public school system. She is now fully retired; yet still open to what God may have in store for her in the future.

Aside from her writings, Valorie loves gardening, collecting and reading inspirational books, traveling, gospel, jazz and oldies music. She considers herself a life-long learner and attends seminars, conferences and conventions. She also gives presentations on self-care and stress management for the caregiver (or anyone).

Her favorite scriptures are Psalm 23, and the Book of Proverbs. Her favorite hymns are "His Eye is on the Sparrow" and "We'll Understand it Better By and By." Aspiring to become the person God would have her become, Valorie tries to be an inspiration to everyone she meets. Her motto is, "Helping others from day to day as I journey along life's way."

Commit to the Lord whatever you do and your plans will succeed. – Proverb 16:3 (NIV)

CPSIA information can be obtained
at www.ICGtesting.com
Printed in the USA
LVHW010717261222
735925LV00005B/293

9 798985 279702